The Minor Key

The Minor Key

Books by Richard Jones

The Minor Key
Paris
Avalon
Stranger on Earth
The Obscure Hours: Translations
The King of Hearts
The Correct Spelling & Exact Meaning
Apropos of Nothing
The Blessing: New & Selected Poems
The Stone It Lives On
48 Questions
The Abandoned Garden
A Perfect Time
At Last We Enter Paradise
Sonnets
Country of Air
Walk On
Innocent Things
Windows and Walls

The Minor Key

poems

Richard Jones

Green Linden Press

Green Linden Press
208 Broad Street South
Grinnell, Iowa 50112
www.greenlindenpress.com

Library of Congress Cataloging-in-Publication Data
Names: Jones, Richard, author.
Title: The Minor Key : poems / Richard Jones.
Description: Grinnell, Iowa : Green Linden Press, 2021
Identifiers: LCCN 2021940528 | ISBN 9781737162513 (paperback)
Subjects: LCGFT : Poetry.
Classification: LCC PS3560.O52475 2021 | DDC 811/.54–dc23
LC record available at https://lccn.loc.gov/2021940528

Cover art: *Spring in Gościeradz* by Leon Wyczółkowski
Book design: Sabrina Szos & Christopher Nelson
Text set in Adobe Garamond Pro & Josefin Sans

Green Linden Press is a nonprofit publisher dedicated to fostering excellent poetry and supporting reforestation with a portion of proceeds.

Acknowledgments

The American Journal of Poetry: "Goodbye," "Heaven," "Operator"

The Cape Rock: "Gray"

Change Seven: "The Train"

Cloudbank: "The Great Sorrow," "Love Poem," "Marbles," "Promised Land," "Suffering," "Tidying Up as a Spiritual Exercise," "Time"

Cultural Weekly: "Long-Distance Call to My Mother," "Money," "Two Martinis"

The Elevation Review: "Optimist"

Escape into Life: "The Grail," "Kansas City," *La Liste,* "Midnight: 19 Below Zero," "One day he decided he wanted to live," "The Photographer," "The Sonnet Is Always a Love Poem," "The Temple," "Truth," "Tuesday," "Z"

Gargoyle: "The Hayrick"

GFT Press: "Melancholy," "Wonders"

Grand Little Things: "The Phonograph," "A Villanelle"

The Hamilton Stone Review: "Daughter," "Jeu de Paume," "Star Route One"

Hiram Poetry Review: "Water"

Hole in the Head Review: "The Little Girl"

Impermanent Earth: "The Moonfaced Coyote"

The Louisville Review: "The Conspiracy," "Youth"

New World Writing: "Alzheimer's," "Boxing in a Backyard Ring on a Summer Night"

Poet Lore: "The Photograph"

Smartish Pace: "Tramp Steamer"

Speckled Trout Review: "The Best Meal"

Star 82 Review: "Czechoslovakia," "Elephants," "Save Yourself"

Thrush: "Bookmarks"

The 2River View: "The Gospel," "A Little Blessing"

Under a Warm Green Linden: "The Fortune-Teller," "Painting at Night," "The Study," "True Country"

upstreet: "On Flying," "The Reader," "Would You Like to See Jupiter?"

Valley Voices: "The Nap," "Thoreau," "Trying to Drive"

The Wallace Stevens Journal: "*A* and *The*"

West Trade Review: "India"

Contents

for the tunesmiths

The Minor Key

E minor

ma chandelle est morte

Love Poem

If it were Valentine's Day and I in jail
and in love with the jailer's daughter,
I'd write a letter
praising her brown eyes and long black hair.
From behind bars I'd remind her
that in spite of these chains,
my spirit is free
and that the best words in my heart
blossom because of her.
I'd write my letter on plain paper
with an ink pen,
but it would be as marvelous
as if I'd written on papyrus
with a feather quill.
If pardoned,
I'd ask the hard-hearted jailer for his daughter's hand.
She and I would live as one
in a room not much bigger than my cell
and we'd walk through town
and comfort those in pain,
the poor in spirit and the downtrodden.
Then I'd lie with my bride in protest
on the marble steps of the temple of justice,
the white stone, warmed by the sun, hot and angry
against our skin.

The Train

We're all on the train
to oblivion, so let's
ride in the noisy bar

or take a high seat
in the observation car
and count the small towns

or simply enjoy
the music of wheels rolling
underneath us,

the comforting sound
of the tracks that point one way,
the sudden darkness

of tunnels through hills
and then the strong light that comes
as we drowse and doze

or turn the pages
of a novel we're anxious
to finish reading before

we arrive,
slowing to a stop
at the terminal

where we all depart,
home at the end of the track,
stepping off the train

and now carrying
nothing in our hands, no bags,
only our brief lives

like an old black coat
we throw over our shoulders
in case it gets cold.

Goodbye

I was accustomed to heavy boots
caked in mud, so I had to let go
when a quick wind got under me
and billowed my coat like a sail
and lifted me like a hot-air balloon.
I confess I was confused but also
delighted, even though I had
no idea what was going on. Really
there was nothing for me to do
but enjoy the freedom of floating
over the town with its slate roofs,
stone church and bell tower,
maze of lanes and snuggle ways
and shops with flower boxes, out
across meadows of timothy and
alfalfa and hedgerows of hawthorn,
and then along the rocky seacoast,
the relentless surf crashing white
at the base of the high cliffs
where I sailed like a lone gull
on the updrafts over the headlands.
The sun spoke my name plainly
in a language that was so serious
it took a good deal of hovering
and soaring in big fluffy clouds
before I finally understood what
was being said. I had been called
and there was no time for goodbyes.

Elephants

I wouldn't mind hallucinating—
it's such a quiet day in the house
with nothing going on that a few
colorful visions would be a welcome
distraction from the curse of ennui.
I learned the word *ennui* in college
and that ennui could kill a man
if he were a French existentialist.
Maybe if I suddenly gave up drinking
I would come down with a case of
delirium tremens. I'd get the shakes
and see white mice and pink elephants—
a herd of pink elephants thundering
toward me sitting in my easy chair.
Led by the wise old matriarch,
they parade before me, trunk to tail,
with hardly a glance my way, as if
I were some lonely bull elephant,
one of those high-savanna drifters
who long ago went off by himself
to live a solitary and quiet existence.

On Flying

I do it so often in my dreams,
sometimes I wake in the morning
and expect to open the door and fly
to the university where I teach.
I'd lead the class up to the roof
and show my students how it is done.
For dramatic effect, I'd climb onto a ledge
and balance—though no one needs a high ledge
or even a rooftop to fly. As a joke
I'd wet my finger to test the wind
because the wind doesn't matter either.
Then I'd become deadly serious
and tell them to watch closely
as I'd lift into the air and begin flying
above the campus sycamores,
all because of the slightest, almost
imperceptible bounce in my step.

Save Yourself

But first I must save the others—
the goldfish swimming in their little glass ocean;
the ficus too weary to carry its greenness any further,
surrendering all hope
and dropping its leaves;
and the little terrier dying of hunger, her brown eyes begging—

and so I go to the upstairs apartment—
the vacationing tenants gone,
the key to their locked door entrusted to me—
and minister the eucharist of the doggy treat
and scatter fish food into the fishbowl, the dusty flakes
falling from my fingers like a blessing of manna.
Then I bring the window garden back to life
with rain that I pour from an old tin cup.

The Conspiracy

The Sisters of Charity were suddenly in my house,
going through the rooms, emptying the cupboards
and closets of any and every thing that was wretched
and wrong, gathering my hatefulness in their arms

and carrying it to the yard, where a pile of ugliness
grew to astonishing proportions. One of the Sisters
stepped forward and with the tiniest wooden match
set the horrible mountain on fire, a great ghastly pyre

that illumined the unworldly faces and lowly white habits.
I could see it was a conspiracy against my selfishness,
my meager vision of the world and what love means,
and found myself at a high window, knocking on the pane

and calling down for the Sisters to come back inside.
There was still much to do—the attic and the basement.

The Nap

Some people are violently opposed
to the idea of a nap. They see a nap—
that gentle midday rest and snooze—
as a waste of good sunlight or, worse,
a sign of sloth, decadence, even moral
decay. "One must work while it is day,
for the night is coming when no man
will work." Fair enough, but even Jesus
took his disciples away to a quiet place
so they could rest their heads on stones
in the shade beneath a bright blue sky.
As one who welcomes a daily siesta,
I forgive the stern judgments of those
who are ever awake and vigilant.
More, I thank them for staying awake,
knowing they are keeping watch
and will shake me should the Lord return.
Then at the blast of the final trumpet,
I will quickly rise from my comfy sofa,
open-eyed and ready to be raptured,
the very thing I dream of on sleepy afternoons
when I drowse and doze in my heaven of pillows.

Alzheimer's

I dress my mother matter-of-factly.
She sits on the side of her bed
and I lift off her blue nightgown
and replace her underpants
with fresh ones. I pull around her
a cream-colored bra, then a white blouse
with a collar. I roll her knee socks up her legs
and then pull onto her the smart black slacks
she still loves. I put on her left tennis shoe first,
then her right, and double-knot them.
I bring a navy sweater over her head
and arrange it, pulling the blouse collar
through the V-neck so she looks put together.
I comb her white hair with a brush as gently as I can,
without hurrying, before I touch her lips
with the lipstick she's worn forever—a Revlon
color that makes her pale, wan skin glow
and is aptly named Cherries in the Snow.
When we're all done, I offer her my arm
and hand her the cane. I say, "Let's go, Beautiful,"
then I escort her to the kitchen where
we drink coffee together, looking
out the window without saying a word
to each other, but we're happy,
if *happy* is the word for the way this feels.

The Phonograph

I was five when my father opened the Telefunken
console stereo and showed me how it was done—

slip the LP from its colorful cardboard cover
and, with open palms, hold the disc like a lover

and fit the center hole over the silver spindle.
Volume was key. It was best not to over-fiddle

with the dials. Keep all knobs in the middle,
like little clocks tolling noon or midnight.

The flat record waited on its round rubber mat
as I held my breath and pressed Start. That

lifted the tonearm, which swung like a crane
but gently, gentler than a drop of rain,

it dropped the diamond needle on a single groove.
The turntable began its sophisticated move

and after a long moment—a scratch and hiss—
my father looked me in the eye and said, "This—

this is Count Basie. This is sublime."
And he snapped his cool fingers, teaching me time.

Time

Had I lived two hundred years ago
I would have played violin in the evening,
and when I sat by a window to read a leather volume
I'd pour myself a glass of sherry.
In winter there would have been a stone fireplace,
a blazing hearth where five big dogs sleep,
dogs who accompany me on long country walks.
I may not have been rich, but I wouldn't have been ashamed
of my tweed overcoat and tall black boots.
My son tells me he'd have worn a military uniform,
a navy jacket with gold buttons, epaulettes, medals and braids,
red-striped trousers and a gilded scabbard.
As an engraver's apprentice and part-time blacksmith,
I say I prefer a vest with a gold chain and watch fob
with an inscribed pocket watch to heft and open
so that with a flick and a glance I would know
exactly what time it was, the face and arrow hands
telling me whether I was in the right century.
Right century or not, I'd spend my free time painting,
wearing a long cotton smock and blue wool pants,
taking all the time I needed at my easel
to really look and see the vase of flowers.
Some days I may have gone without food
in order to buy paints, inks, paper, and books.
And nights when I wasn't painting or reading or playing violin,
I'd sit at my desk and write. I'd light two tall candles
and become one with the violet ink and linen paper,
my steel pen and nib dancing to the music of time.

Boxing in a Backyard Ring on a Summer Night

Beckett is younger, the far superior fighter with
every advantage in skill, timing, and technique.
A bricklayer by trade, his gloved fists are stones,
and his hard, solid punches rock me on my heels.
Sometimes a blow is concussive, as if some brute
has bashed me in the head with a small boulder,
then the world goes away. When it comes back,
I have no idea where I am. I stand inside my skull
like standing in a marble dome or a cathedral.
When I retreat to my corner, I sit on a little stool,
where my imaginary trainer throws water on my face
and my imaginary manager screams, "Cross his right!
Circle to the left! Stay away from his jab!" Reeling,
I spit blood in a bucket. Far off a little bell rings,
and like warriors we stand and box another round,
rescuing what's been lost. This life is interminable—
the way that he'll always be there waiting for me,
his fists raised, never backing away, moving forward—
sixty seconds counted down by a plastic egg timer
and the desire to knock a man senseless.

Marbles

To think I once believed I'd wake a new man—
my spirit and all my thoughts enlightened.
Imagine how surprised I was to discover
I was young again, a little blond boy of five.

My spirit and all my thoughts enlightened,
I was kneeling in a circle of dirt, shooting marbles.
Imagine how surprised I was to discover
the steady hand and perfect aim of a real shooter.

I was kneeling in a circle of dirt, shooting marbles
with Socrates, Augustine, and George Harrison.
The steady hand and perfect aim of a real shooter,
each had become a kneeling child, playing.

With Socrates, Augustine, and George Harrison,
I was young again, a little blond boy of five.
Each had become a kneeling child, playing.
To think I once believed I'd wake a new man!

Kansas City

I want to go to Kansas City.
In all my long life, I've never met anyone
who's actually been there.
It makes me wonder if Kansas City really exits.
I've read Ernest Hemingway,
born in Oak Park, Illinois, in 1899,
wrote for the city's newspaper,
the *Kansas City Star*.
But does anyone really believe that?
I mean, who names a newspaper the *Star*?
I say it's all just the stuff of imagination,
the fabric of poetry, like Valhalla or Parnassus.
As a teenager, I heard the poet on the radio
longing to stand on Twelfth Street and Vine.
His song was so sad—
I knew he'd never go to Kansas City.
I knew he'd never find a crazy little woman
who'd love him with all his problems.
As for me, I can't say exactly how I'm going
to get there. I might take a train.
I might take a plane. But even if I have to walk,
well, just the same, even with these old legs, I'm going.
I mean it. I'm really going to go to Kansas City.
I know it may be a rich, far-fetched dream,
and such things don't happen
or ever come true,
but think about it—
Kansas City…
Even the Beatles wanted to go there.

Tramp Steamer

The idea was to steal away—
slip down to the harbor
where the foreign ships docked,
find an unfamiliar flag
on a rusted tramp ship
about to weigh anchor,
and bribe the captain.
As midnight buoys
rocked and clanged—
like church bells
announcing a death—
I'd hoist my rucksack,
climb the gangplank,
and like a nameless ghost
vanish in swirls of mist.
I'd hole up in a cheap cabin
reeking of oil
above the engine room
and while the ship
(carrying guns)
made course southward
for some unknown destination,
I'd lie quiet in an anonymous berth,
turning the pages
of dime novels,
pretending to read.
The idea was to keep to myself,
stay sober, abstain
from cards and dice,
avoid being stabbed
or poisoned.
Storms and rough seas

were to be expected;
burst gaskets and hull leaks
would be routine.
I'd ask no questions,
answer no questions.
The idea was to say
little or nothing,
to stand alone and mortal
on the bridge under stars
and think only of freedom.
I would be a wraith,
as insubstantial as air,
and survive the voyage
by observing the crew,
secretly noting which
among the rootless sailors
were deserters,
opium eaters, swindlers,
saboteurs, or spies,
taking special care with the spies
because a spy must be ruthless,
deceitful to survive.
To protect himself,
to remain concealed,
a spy would as soon kill you
as look at you,
even if you were nobody,
just some lonely soul
who had simply had enough of the world.

Czechoslovakia

Though the country no longer exists,
Czechoslovakia is the code word
my wife and I employ when we are
with other people. At a dinner party,
should I turn to the host and ask,
"Have you visited Czechoslovakia?"
my wife knows I am breaking—
that I'm in trouble and need to leave.
"Czechoslovakia" means all the glass
is beginning to shatter. Even when we
lie in bed, quiet and intimate, some nights
my wife will decipher my inner thoughts.
"Where are you?" she'll say. And I'll say,
"I'm lost somewhere in the dark woods
of Czechoslovakia and can't get home."

One day he decided he wanted to live

in Vienna, to waste the summer musing,
maybe all of autumn too, drinking sweet
tea in cafés and eating Sacher torte, listening
to Mozart and Brahms. He took a tour
of Freud's house and wanted to lie down
on the famous sofa and tell the doctor
his dreams and who his mother was.
Walking the avenues in the twilight,
he could not explain, but found charming,
the system of symbols the world became.
Sometimes he would jot foreign phrases,
he would whisper for their exquisite sound.
When winter came to his narrow room,
he wrote many elegies for the Viennese light.

Water

The hour was late, the house quiet,
my wife asleep, my mind restless.
My daughter, sick with the flu,
was still up, writing a research
paper about water for English class.
Water, she said, covered the planet—
our streams, lakes, oceans, and ice caps.
We are made of water, she typed.
I'd carried a pitcher of water upstairs
to slake her thirst and slay her fever.
After I kissed dreaming wife and writing-
in-spite-of-illness daughter good night,
I sat in the dark and took a little sip too,
hoping the cool water might help me
make it through the night until tomorrow,
vowing to rise and go forth and lend a hand,
a calm mind flowing from a deep source
the way water flows from a pure spring—
first in a tiny trickle, then as a mighty river.

The Best Meal

From bowls of fire, we spooned blue flames,
tiny infernos surprisingly sweet and cool,
the flavor unlike any we'd known, tasting
of evening sky and rain. Our five senses
were all heightened when our host's words
made us believe everything is true and real,
like work and sleep, or how the back hurts
after a day in the garden. And we grew quiet
as he told stories about loss and darkness,
about blessings left by the side of the road.
Many had gathered at the table, all hungry
for knowledge, all of us famished for faith—
wisdom more satisfying than the intoxicating
flames we lifted with spoons to our mouths.

D minor

the silence of a falling star lights up a purple sky

Promised Land

Before the sun comes up
I slip out of the blue tent
and stir the night's embers
into a fire to make coffee,
the woods blue with mist.
I like the way the air feels
to breathe, the dew heavy
on my shoulders as I slice
bacon and open a can of beans
to cook in a heavy iron skillet.
The campfire's blue smoke
climbs the steep hill
past a sliver of moon
caught in the branches,
past the fast stream singing
a song about snowmelt,
the icy water on my face
a kind of pure wakefulness
I welcome and will carry
all day as I climb, packing
only some bread, a canteen,
and a poncho for storms.
Dawn is coming, the coffee
is almost ready, the small fire
crackles in its circle of stones,
and already I feel I've climbed
to the high outcrop of granite
and that I'm looking out over
the green roof of the forest
and the blue lake in the distance
stretching all the way to Canada.

The Little Girl

After her father died,
she still had to go
back to school. The first
day after the funeral
there was a big snow.
Early in the morning
I drove slowly from
my house up the lane
to the house where
she lived and now
stood alone without
her mother in a big
drift at the lane's end
waiting for the bus.
The white lane was icy
and I drove dreamily
as a black hearse, slow
enough for each of us
to catch the other's
eye and to silently
wave hello, hello,
and for me to note
the way she seemed
remote and far away,
snowflakes gracing
the shoulders of her
blue wool overcoat like
small circles of cut lace.

A Little Blessing

Butterfly suffers
from anxiety attacks
and puffy Sparrow
weeps sadly because
her mate did not return
to the white birdhouse
and she does not know
what's become of him.
Grasshopper confesses
he's addicted to clover.
Fox whispers he never tells
the truth, pleasant or bad.
But it's okay, they tell me,
there is good news—
the sun is shining today
and the breeze is warm.
Butterfly opens her wings
but does not fly away—
instead flutters and graces
my shoulder. Sparrow
takes a little hop toward me
and Grasshopper and Fox
come closer too. Together
we all join in a benediction
and I thank them for their blessing,
for their kindness and goodness,
as if I were Saint Francis
and we were all together
on a sunny hillside in Assisi
in the world of ten thousand joys
and ten thousand sorrows.

Wonders

> *Then glut thy sorrow*
> *on a morning rose.*
>   —John Keats

Apparently, I too glut my sorrow
with the wonders of this world—
white stones and red jaspers,
a brown cattail and purple tulip petals,
the blue vane of a feather,
the bow and blade of a skeleton key,
a tuning fork, a pitch pipe,
a plumb line and wooden level,
magnifying glass and microscope,
a trustworthy weathervane arrowhead,
an hourglass of sand, compass and needle,
and also silver needle, thimble, and thread,
hinge and hasp, chain and pulley—
all lined up in front of my books
or randomly arranged on the shelves,
small wonders I inventoried
and catalogued this morning
as I climbed the bookshelf ladder
to retrieve the dusty book I needed.

Melancholy

I write of melancholy
to avoid melancholy.
—Robert Burton

I climbed the bookshelf ladder this morning
to retrieve the dusty book I needed,
Robert Burton's *Anatomy of Melancholy*,
a nine-hundred-page tome published in 1621,
a treatise on those small occasions
of sorrow, need, anguish, dullness, and fear.
Stepping back down, I remembered
The Anatomy was John Keats's favorite book.
Balancing on the ladder,
Burton's heavy volume tucked in my arm,
I reached also for *The Poems*
with Keats's name in gold letters on the spine.
I lingered a moment on the step
and remembered that in "Ode on Melancholy"
Joy is forever bidding adieu.
No argument there, my friend.
Keats says a fit of melancholy can fall
"Sudden from heaven like a weeping cloud"—
and that the only thing a man can do
is taste "the sadness" of Melancholy's might.
By the time I finally climbed down
and had carried the books to my desk,
I already knew that Keats and Burton
were in the room with me, their spirits
sitting beside me and helping my hand
compose a poem about all the small wonders
arranged on my bookshelves, which celebrate life.

Two Martinis

I fill a glass pitcher with ice
and ponder *which gin to pour?*
The Tanqueray and Beefeater,
Bombay Sapphire and Hendrick's,
along with bottles of whiskey and rye,
other sundry liquors and orange bitters,
line up like blue and brown books,
everything stored out of the light behind
two shuttered doors that hide the little
alcove bar's shelves of glasses, sink,
marble lamp, and champagne bucket.
Today I pour a clear cup of immaculate,
organic gin called Art of the Still
from Trader Joe's where I buy
the cheap cabernets I sip when writing.
I take two glasses from the freezer,
the cups frosted, and slip a half jigger
of dry vermouth into the V of each
before swirling and pouring it out,
the sheen a thing of beauty to behold.
(At Christmas I rinse the glasses with
Cointreau to make the glass gleam.)
I stir the pitcher slowly with a long glass
wand to mix and melt the gin and ice,
stirring delicately not to bruise the gin,
then pour the glass full and adorn the rim
with a long twist of lemon for my wife,
mine being dirty with a splash of brine
and a cocktail skewer with three olives.
I wave the vermouth bottle over the drinks
like a final blessing and call my wife,
who after a long day needs the taste

of winter and juniper and icy sunlight
more than I do. Together we lift our martinis
and hold them aloft for as long as we can,
just thinking about the alchemy of cocktails.
See us touch our glasses and take a sip,
the dainty gesture more refined than a kiss?

The Moonfaced Coyote

The moonfaced coyote
napping in the compost,
the fox trotting by the hedge
with a rabbit in its mouth,
the family of five deer
who daily graze the hostas,
not to mention the birds—
woodpeckers, jays, robins,
orioles, finches, cardinals,
the ruby-throated hummingbird
one could mistake for a sprite,
a little spirit come to save us,
even ducks and herons and hawks—
even white and blue butterflies,
and the squirrels and chipmunks
who act as if they are the central
characters in an animated musical,
the low croaking songs of frogs,
the din of cicadas and crickets,
and evening's lightning bugs
whose Morse code spells *hope*,
the night's swirling bats feeding
on tiny moths and mosquitoes
that spin in the purple twilight,
the owl perched on a low branch
contemplating everything and
the curious hands of the masked
raccoon looking for something
to steal, something to feast on,
while in the wee hours three mice
get away with anything they want
in the quiet of the dimly lit kitchen,

and then, not least and never last,
the elegant skunk parading his black
fur like a prince or perfumed dandy
on the moonlit lawn, its silky stripe
a white banner of goodness and purity
as it dines all night below my window
on a banquet of beetles and grubs.

A and *The*

If you want to write poetry,
all you need to know is the difference
between the indefinite and definite article

and how the choice a poet makes
directs the reader's imagination
deeper into the mystery of things.

A door versus *the* door; *the* road
rather than *a* road; *a* house, no, *the* house—
how quickly the little words show us the way.

It may not be the spiraling universe
in a grain of sand, but down through the years
it's a lesson I've shared with my students,

a worthy summation of all one needs
to pick up a pen and write. Beyond that,
the question is how to get on with a life.

Z

The letter *Z*
has all the zeal I need—

from zero
to zenith

I find my Zen
and my Zion,

my zither
and my zinnias,

my gadzooks
and my zonked-out zeppelin,

the zoot suit I'll wear
when life zigzags

from Zimbabwe
to Zurich.

Optimist

Tomorrow will be a good day,
and the day after tomorrow
will be even better.

Next Wednesday also looks promising,
and the first of the month
looms on the horizon like a ship of gold.

I think next year will be the best year of my life
and that each following year will surely
outdo the one before.

From where I'm sitting today,
a decade from now looks like
nirvana

and eternity—
I can see it—
is overflowing with fountains of light.

A Villanelle

I will never write a villanelle—
the French have a different kind of voice.
Though villanelles are loved in both heaven and hell,

I write sonnets instead. Sonnets tell
stories full of complications and choice.
I will never write a villanelle

because their refrains tend to spell
the theme too loudly, like nails pounded into a joist.
Though villanelles are loved in both heaven and hell,

I tend toward free verse and the little bell
of internal rhyme that rings when a rhythm is in poise.
I will never write a villanelle

as I will never sculpt in marble—
freeing a song from the white stone's noise.
Though villanelles are loved in both heaven and hell,

I shall remain happy with my crystal
couplets and all my Shakespearean joys.
I will never write a villanelle,
though villanelles are loved in both heaven and in hell.

Bookmarks

How to Make a Coffin, How to Bake Madeleines,
Color Standards and Color Nomenclature, Gravity,
Readings in Theravada Buddhism, Gardens, Preparing
Your Last Will and Testament, Fly-Fishing, The Puritans,
Aristotle's Six Elements of Drama, The Way of the Cross,
Wood for Making Violins, The Salt Satyagraha, Heaven,
British Museum Reading Room, The Language of Flowers,
Knowledge of the Holy, Paintings of the Louvre, Incense,
Exorcisms and Healing Miracles, The Communist Manifesto,
The Villa Borghese, Zen, Depression and Suicide, Mother
Teresa, The Flight Physiology of a Bird, Brain Function,
The Moon and Madness, Revelation Sermons, Insomnia,
The Great Wave, Monet and Blindness, The Fullness of Time,
The End of the World, How to Survive in the Wilderness.

Gray

The color of storm skies
        or a riverbed of stones
a girl's eyes in the morning
        or the air inside a cave

the color of winter rain
        or a worn gravel path
the dull lead in a pencil
        and the suicide note

old coins on a table
        the preacher's wedding band
the key in an orphan's hand
        the feel of a broken promise

the fog-hidden mountain
        the misty fallow fields
a low garden wall
        a modest country cottage

the weathered latch
        and the lament and song
of the broken hinge
        when the gate is opened

La Liste

When I climb the stairs, dragging
all my cares behind me like a
bag of thorns and shattered glass,
I find Voltaire in my bed, sleeping,
his thick reading glasses still on,
head propped on feather pillows,
his white nightcap slightly askew,
an open book in his hands waiting
in the eerie glow of the green lamp
for an arthritic finger to turn a page.
The French have a clean conscience
and sleep as soundly as the dead
while I sit wide-awake in a red chair.
Though he's gently snoring, I need
to talk to him, and in halting French
I ask about his life, his victories,
whispering to the dreaming writer
the way one whispers to the departed
when keeping a lonely night's vigil.
I remind Voltaire that Dostoyevsky said,
"Man is fond of reckoning up his troubles,"
and then from my shirt pocket take
a long list written in pencil of life's
troubles and adversities, a list of woes
that I translate into passable French
and read aloud as if I were reciting
a kindhearted and melodious poem
the sleeping old writer might love.

Trying to Drive

On a crowded highway, I try to steer
and unfold the map, remembering that
according to Buddhist cartography,
many realms of life may be explored
within the sphere of consciousness.
By my calculations, I must be lost
in the Realm of Hungry Ghosts—
for lately it seems my mind is all desire
and my spiritual longing never satisfied.
The Buddha would lift a gentle hand
and stop me in the road. He'd explain
the heavenly realms and enlighten me
never to confuse torment and rapture.
But he's the Buddha and his journey
has arrived at its perfectly still center,
while I'm on the expressway with cars
lined up behind me and honking because
I'm disoriented and driving too slowly,
map in tatters. Even a plodding trailer
passes me by, its bumper sticker saying:
You can follow me if you will, but I'm lost too.

Truth

People don't believe it when I tell them once
I was sentenced to six months on the chain gang.
My friends and I were sixteen. In the courtroom
that day, the hanging judge pounded his gavel,
delivered his verdict, instructed the town deputy
to take us away, but that didn't happen because
our parents immediately stood, outraged, yelling,
all the parents in the gallery protesting the verdict,
all save my mother, who'd fainted to her knees.
The fathers stretched her out as on a church pew
and shook their fists at the old man on the bench.
Hearing this story, people say I embellish. I say no,
it all turned out all right. In something the law calls
Prayer for Judgment, the judge released us boys
with a final commandment: as long as we never
transgressed in North Carolina again, we need not
suffer condemnation or endure the harsh sentence.
I'm a witness to the truth. Still, people scoff and smirk
and like Pilate they always ask, "And what is truth?"

Jeu de Paume

Why can I not remember such a remarkable Monday—
June 17 in sunny Paris in 1974 when I was twenty
and toured the Jeu de Paume with the girl I loved
(who looked like the girl in Renoir's *La Liseuse*).

I still have the daily diary I wrote that records our visit,
and to this day in my study over my desk the cheap print
I bought of Van Gogh's blue church hangs, a painting
I've looked at every morning for nearly half a century.

The Jeu de Paume was perhaps the greatest museum ever—
crowded with paintings by Degas, Monet, Gauguin,
Morisot, Manet, Sisley, Pissarro, Redon, Cézanne—
but it closed in the eighties and the paintings were relocated

to the new Musée d'Orsay. It's strange: I can recall every visit
to the d'Orsay—which masterpieces I pondered and studied
and who accompanied me and also the times I went alone.
But over the decades, the Jeu de Paume's been lost to mind.

In Paris I've since walked past the building without a thought
and try though I will, I cannot retrieve yesteryear's memory;
although I *was* there that day—it's recorded in my own hand.
Perhaps I was overwhelmed by such great art and love—

all those paintings and my sweetheart in one small building!
Maybe it was too much for the young man I was then
to take in and keep, a moment almost too blissful to believe.
All that's left of that long-ago day in Paris is a torn ticket stub
that bookmarks the worn museum catalogue written in French.

The Photograph

In a scarred wooden box in the garage
I found the photograph of the youth
I once was, torn in half from top to bottom.
One half had lain for decades facing down;
one half had waited, all these years,
looking up from the box at the sky.
I lifted the two halves and studied them.
I saw my right hand had been divorced
from the left. I saw a divided mind,
a riven heart. Kneeling in the garage,
I wiped each torn half clean on my sleeve
and joined the two halves of the face.
I regarded the black eyes, their fury
and despair. I held the pieces together.
Instead of dropping the picture back
into the box, I looked more closely.
I was wearing a tattered T-shirt and jeans,
standing by the lilacs in my mother's garden.
Then the torn-in-two boy might have been asking,
Tell me, now that you know—
what should I have done with my life?

Operator

1972

On a late autumn night of rain,
having been on the road for days,
I step inside a telephone booth
along the side of a highway
and pull the door to turn on the light.
Digging in my jeans for quarters and dimes,
I place the coins on the metal ledge,
my long hair dripping, my boots wet.
The rain keeps falling. I don't know
whom to call. My mother? My sister?
An eighteen-wheeler rushes past
and rattles the glass, headlamps scanning
the rainy night scarred by light and dark,
maybe riding for miles on the wrong road.
I lift the black receiver from its cradle,
cradle the receiver against my left ear,
look at the numbers, take a long breath.
I need to put my finger in the rotary,
spin the roulette wheel of the dial,
be still and listen to the phone ringing
and those long silences in between
that are like being in a dark, bottomless pit.
Rain on the metal roof. The white light.
I see the last number on the dial is zero.
Beneath the zero is the word *operator*.
Yes, the operator. I could call the operator.
Maybe the operator will answer.
Maybe the operator will tell me what I should do.

Star Route One

I lived at the end of a dirt road—
a clapboard farmhouse with a big porch,
a ramshackle, make-do place

cobbled together over time under a tin roof.
A letter from home came once a month
addressed simply to Star Route One,

and the only living things I spoke to
were the gentle cows and the horses.
I had everything I could need—

a ramshackle, make-do place,
a big porch, an orchard,
a mind sharp and ready to fight.

I drank well water, ate the food I grew.
I had everything I could need
and the patience to wait for poems

that came each day in every season.
I recorded the words in a blue notebook,
lines that seemed dictated by the wind,

and I had many blue notebooks
and a good supply of pens
so I could revise endlessly,

scratching out lines entire, writing anew,
then typing and retyping. My typewriter
harmonized with rain on the tin roof,

the words, recorded in blue notebooks,
finding their natural music, a minor key.
I remember gazing out the tall study windows,

the orchard in bloom, the pasture abuzz,
the mountains blue and low on the horizon
as I revised endlessly. Typing and retyping

I would look up from my typewriter
and gaze out the tall study windows
to see what was headed my way,

the mountains blue and low on the horizon,
the orchard barren, the pasture in snow.
The dirt road forever empty and still,

the only living things I spoke to
were the gentle cows and the horses.
I practiced patience, mind at the ready.

I drank well water, ate the food I grew.
Looking down the empty dirt road,
I revised endlessly, typing and retyping

because I knew something was coming,
something far better than poems—
something sweet, something good,

something that would last a lifetime.

A minor

my consolation is in the stardust of a song

Heaven

In heaven, carpenters
drop plumb lines
to build mansions
for those yet to come,
and masked physicians
repair broken hearts
in operating rooms
where Bach plays softly.
Fishermen cast lines
over calm, green water;
cooks cook feasts,
and poets in black coats
work on poems
never finished in life.
Look at their pencils
and white manuscripts,
the way they work line
by line to the end.

The Reader

When I walk to the farmers' market
on a sunny Saturday suburban morning,
I walk with an army of conscripts
and volunteers marching two by two—
Jimmie Rodgers and Hank Williams,
John Keats and Rainer Maria Rilke,
Emily and Walt, John and Paul.
The troops walk down Kings Lane
past Pleasant Street and Cole Park
to the tents of the farmers' market
in the cordoned-off parking lot
of Saints Peter and Paul Church.
I tell two vendors who look like
Paul Verlaine and Mary Cassatt,
"The world is fragile and one must fight
to keep this life in balance." I tell them,
"The soldiers are hungry and we are in need
and I am purchasing much corn,
eggs, vegetables, cheese, and meat."
When the company has loaded
the wagons with the rations needed
for the coming winter and long campaign,
the troops form double columns—
Phil and Don, Isaiah and Jeremiah,
Muddy Waters and Howlin' Wolf,
Georgia O'Keeffe and Lucille Clifton.
Carrying sacks of provisions home
on mules and in our haversacks,
our tight band sings tramping songs
the volunteers have composed
during the long and lonely nights.
Sometimes I walk at the front of the line

and sometimes I bring up the rear,
offering words of encouragement.
But this army needs no incentive:
they will stay with me and I with them
to the very end. At each corner
cars wait at the zebra crosswalk
and as we pass marching and singing,
old men on freshly mown lawns
take off their hats to show respect
to those who have answered the call.
When we get back to my house,
campfires burn quietly in the yard
where in bivouacs by the garden
the men and women write letters
or play the harmonica or just dream
inside their blue tents. Sometimes,
standing on the patio and surveying
the soldiers who've come to our aid,
I wonder whether all the generals give thanks
and how it is that I, a lowly cadet,
became a part of such a large
and formidable brigade.

The Great Sorrow

My daughter grows sad on clear nights when
she looks up into the modern sky and discovers
so few stars to guide her, especially compared
to the countless constellations of the Greek skies
that attended loyal Achilles and inspired Homer.
Beyond the horizon, the shimmering city glows,
lighting up the dark, but nonetheless we stand
in the garden, father and daughter, treasuring
one or two stars twinkling faint, wordless alarms.
The universe, destined to become darker still,
may bring a future with no silver suns at all
to shine down at night and bless us. Soon
only the two of us will praise the darkness,
shining as best we know how, brightly together.

Suffering

Because my doorbell is broken—
it's been on the fritz for months—
the Buddha had to rap many times
with the brass knocker to get my attention.
I don't remember whether I was napping
or working—they are pretty much
the same thing—but opening the door
I recognized the old boy immediately.
I mean, who wouldn't? The guy looks
just the way you'd expect him to look,
that big jiggly belly and saffron robe.
Not knowing what best to say, I said,
"Can I help you?" He replied, "I'm here
to remind you of the first noble truth."
"The truth that life is suffering?" I said,
my tone, I must confess, a bit sarcastic.
I mean, I didn't have to sit under a tree
for eight years to figure that one out.
"Yes," he said. "Suffering. But it's time
for you to transcend all pain and sorrow."
"Right," I said, inviting him in the house
and leading him toward the tiny kitchen.
I put the red kettle on for tea and we sat
together at the small table, talking all day
about what such a thing would mean for me.

True Country

The deliciousness of pain
always surprises me.
Lying in the unmown grass in the backyard
and looking up through a lacework of branches
at swiftly sailing, low-lying, purple-black clouds
that blot out the sunlight,
I find I am looking forward to the coming rain.
A weather depression brings storms
and high winds. The dark will come early
and white candles will light the house
when the power goes out. Inside
I'll sip red wine,
and when the electricity comes back
to make myself whole
I'll drop the needle
on some scratched, well-played blues records,
songs that pine about really loving someone
who leaves you one day for no good reason.
Sadness is being broken like that—
and it's a long, slow torture that lasts a lifetime,
the falling out of love. Such agony is exquisitely empty
but you can sing about it in words with a guitar,
how loneliness is the palace of night
and pain the true country.

The Grail

> *My madness came upon me*
> *as of old.*

After a day of getting nowhere,
I leave my desk at night's end
and find her tranquilly lounging in bed.
I sit on the edge
and with great effort remove one sock.
Most of us would follow wandering fires, I say,
thinking to explain myself.
Propped on a fluffy pillow,
reading her magazine, turning glossy pages,
sipping a glass of white wine,
she never presses the advantage.
She simply pats the white pillow beside her,
calling me to rest.
This earth I walk on
seems not earth,
I confess,
misquoting Tennyson,
pulling back the covers
and dropping the other sock.
Head on my pillow,
I turn to her and see she is in another country
where words have no currency,
though words are all a poet has,
especially when it's late
and the day is lost and
what I saw was veil'd and cover'd
and my feet are cold,
barefoot in blue pajamas.

Tidying Up as a Spiritual Exercise

Suddenly we were ransacking the rooms,
plundering the closets for the skeletons
hanging there. We took the jangly bones
in our arms and carried them dangling and
clattering out to the van, already crammed with
trunks of clothes, cases of books, and boxes
filled with all the little things we once loved.
The hollow skulls gazed through the windows
and the skeletons seemed sad to say goodbye,
but then, in a puff of the muffler's blue smoke,
all that old stuff we never knew what to do with
was gone. Our home was peaceful as a temple
of prayer. It was as if we had freed little lambs
or opened wooden cages and let doves fly.

The Gospel

In spite of the foul tenements and gutters,
in spite of the fact no one is listening
amid the din and desolation,
the anonymity and estrangement,
some truths still slip through the gate
disguised as dreams or anxious poems
or a sudden look. At the flea market
tattered photographs saved in boxes
will be sold to anyone with a few coins,
along with postcards from the past
with the good news shared in faded ink.
Many are afraid, many have lost hope,
yet the old ideas keep getting through—
a suitcase full of leaves, a violin with
a human voice, eyes quick with candle flame.
At night cold pipes clang coded messages
of joy and light in the meaningless dark.

India

I'm not going to make the pilgrimage.
I'm not going to bathe in the Ganges
or walk the Taj Mahal's Garden of Heaven.

I'm just going to lie on the hardwood floor,
drunk on wine and virtue, and almost happy,
a rolled black coat under my head like a pillow.

I cannot be a child once more in my father's yard,
listening to him tell me of how, during the war,
he visited the Taj Mahal and watched holy men

tending funeral pyres on the banks of the Mata Ganga.
I can't gather leaves from the autumn lawn and burn
them at twilight, leaning on the wood-handled rake.

No, there is not time left to visit the Golden Temple,
to walk there without my shoes, or to sleep
in the Himalayas, abode of the clouds. Instead,

tomorrow I'll weed the garden. Or maybe not.
Lying here, I love the weight of wine in my mouth.
When I roll over, I love how the empty blue bottles roll with me.

Tuesday

I invited a sad friend to visit the temple
and see the big, blue pot of begonias behind
the hostas, painted ferns, and tall daylilies,
to smell the sweet, green leaves of the sumac
blessing the midday shadows and breezes.
My friend asked if I were talking of the temple
I'd toured when I was young in faraway Japan.
I said no, I mean the humble paradise I've made
of my backyard garden of roses and boxwood.
It's hard labor, I said, but any garden can be
a living temple. Then if we must leave home,
the garden's fragrant peace accompanies us.
My friend agreed. Yes, he said, he would visit
on Tuesday, and he'd bring his broken heart.

The Fortune-Teller

"I see a farm bathed in moonlight,
an orchard's shadows, a freshwater pond
shining in the dark like black glass,
a painted rowboat on the bank's grass.

I see all the ways you will be blessed—
days wandering the mountain path,
two loyal dogs always by your side,
Labradors named Mercy and Grace.

I see no big mistakes, no small missteps,
no shattered mind, no broken soul,
only dew sparkling on the blue flowers
and guardian angels in the tall pine trees.

I see a house, open windows, white curtains.
I see you thank the night for its compassion."

Money

Then one day money grew on trees,
flowering as dollar bills, oddly enough.
George Washington looked befuddled
hanging like a pear or an almond
from millions of branches in thousands
of orchards. And at night, coins fell
like hail, making all kinds of noise
and denting the hoods of new cars.
At lunch in the cafeteria, if you bit
into an apple you'd find a silver dollar.
Money fell like snow on the mountains—
great drifts and avalanches of bills.
India's Ganges and London's Thames
flooded their banks with currency notes,
soggy pictures of Gandhi and the Queen.
Flemish fields flowered with francs.
The one hundred cents of the euro
became as ubiquitous as grass,
the yen as common as rice.
The dunes of the Sahara and Kalahari?
Sun-dappled powdery flakes of gold
for as far as a caravan could travel!
Even the trash cans of New York City
overflowed with freshly minted hundreds.
There was so much money in such abundance,
money didn't mean the same thing anymore.
It was more like poetry and came naturally,
like the sun in the morning, like leaves to a tree.

The Sonnet Is Always a Love Poem

Driving a silver car from the last millennium
to the high school to pick up my daughter,
I was thinking about a friend who'd traveled
to Switzerland with his father. I don't know

whether they went to Geneva by the blue lake
or to a pristine mountain clinic in the Alps,
but the purpose of the son's trip was to ease
his demented father's assisted suicide. And,

to make the narrative even more unnerving,
his stepmother now refused to live without
her husband. She had appealed to the son
to sign the legal forms so she too could die…

but then I turned into the school parking lot—kids
walking everywhere, singly and in pairs. I had to stay alert.

Long-Distance Call to My Mother

I speak a few words, and then listen.
When silence and terror come between us,
I'm torn: do I speak to reassure her
or give the ruined mind its freedom,
knowing my mother is stubborn
and shall be heard. In her gibberish
and stammering, I hear an iron will,
the desire to say a few clean sentences.
Because I am her son, she trusts me
to translate broken, inarticulate syllables
into questions her heart would ask.
I tell her the good and the bad, knowing
she is strong enough to bear the truth.
And sometimes I say the sweet words,
which she repeats back, enunciating
clearly in her rich accent, a slow drawl
that is like honey warmed by the sun.

The Hayrick

The winter I was seventeen
I took a ten-week battery of psychological
tests at the local college to help figure out my future.
Most kids waffled between medicine and law.
The baffled doctor apologized
when my final results counseled "hermit" or "monk."
I'd never considered becoming a long-robed monk
and didn't think of "hermit" as a legitimate occupation.
I forgot all about careers when I crisscrossed Europe in '74.
I was twenty then and poor
and lived for the moment—Amsterdam, Paris,
the face of the Matterhorn, the fountains of the Alhambra.
I ate little and slept in youth hostels.
I left the Continent in late August,
crossed the channel to London,
and took the train west through Cornwall to Tintagel.
That evening there were no beds left in the hostel.
I walked the village knocking on doors,
but there were no vacant rooms to let
and I hadn't the money anyway.
I walked a narrow lane into the countryside
and in an open field of hayricks
slept on a bed of straw
beneath a sky of English stars.
I'll never forget that night,
listening to the sea crashing below the cliff,
the same eternal sea that crashed in the dark
for Roman soldiers who had ventured to the edge of the world.

Would You Like to See Jupiter?

My neighbor arrives at the front door
and asks would I like to see Jupiter.
The night is clear. I say, Sure, let's
take a look at the god of thunder.
On the front sidewalk Jack sets up
a tripod, aims the long black barrel
of his new SpaceProbe telescope,
and calibrates the small eyepiece.
The night is cool, the jasmine fragrant;
dew shines on the grass like stars.
It only takes a second to look through
a telescope, to see the stripes and swirls,
the undying storm of the Great Red Spot.
Jack and I stand on the lawn like spirits.
A young father and his two daughters
are out for an evening walk. It's so dark
we can't quite make out one another's face.
Hey, we say, would you like to see Jupiter?

The Temple

Segesta, Italy, 1991

I drove my Fiat onto the white ferry
and crossed the Mediterranean to Trapani
where I planned to take the winding road to Segesta.
From the little town tourists like me would board
a big shuttle bus that struggled to climb a narrow
road of switchbacks to the mountaintop temple.
Ticket in hand I crossed the parking lot
and approached the lone shuttle bus.
The sleepy driver spoke no English
but pointed at the watch on his wrist
to tell me it was not yet time. Apparently
the bus climbed exactly on the hour
and it was only quarter past eleven.
I was the only tourist that off-season day,
so there was nothing to do
but speak Italian, a language
I didn't think I knew but that,
after months on the island of Favignana,
issued forth like a song from an opera.
The driver had seemed content to wait,
to sit alone in his big bus and say nothing,
but when out of the blue I began to speak,
asking, "*Ciao, come ti senti oggi, amico mio?*"
the driver's eyes woke up. He cheered me on,
saying my Italian was good, surprisingly good,
molto bene, yes, yes, sì, sì! Inspired, emboldened,
I asked about his life, his country, his family.
I waved my hands in the Italian manner,
like a maestro who wished to emphasize
certain words that were especially important,

such as *motorbike* or *typewriter* or *roof garden*.
When it was finally noon and time to start
the engine and drive up the mountain—
just the two of us—I sat in the front seat,
still talking, still fluttering my hands like birds.
I can still remember as though it were yesterday—
the bus climbs higher and higher,
the Tyrrhenian Sea sparkles in the distance,
and I tell the bus driver everything in Italian,
all about my life and the book I have written:
"I am a writer. I live in a house on the island.
I like to eat. I swim all day. The water is cold.
The night sky is dark with stars like salt.
The country is beautiful. I like the sky.
I very much like the sea and the sky.
Now the temple. Now I am a book of poems."

Thoreau

Like Thoreau, I'm happy to keep things simple—
a manuscript spread on morning's table,
a glass of wine in the garden in the evening.
I could live with just the birds and the trees,
so companionable I find them, ever generous
with trilling songs and cool summer breezes.
Sometimes there is a party to go to in town—
the conversation, the glass of champagne.
Too often I find myself leaning against a wall,
lost in thought, wishing I were home again,
working at my desk or dreaming on my sofa,
rapt in a reverie, like Thoreau in his tiny house,
sitting in his doorway beneath the pines and hickories,
time flowing, the sunlit summer sumacs sparkling.

Midnight: 19 Below Zero

Because the house is so quiet, so cold,
I take each of the three guitars in turn
and by the fire's radiant coals
play my son William's amber Strat
to keep it warm, full of life and love,
next, taking special care with my 1964
Silver Fox Epiphone—my childhood guitar—
then, while leaden moonlight falls on
roofs piled with snow, sing and strum
Sarah's acoustic, playing folk and country
until the guitar's richly mellow as the sun.
Now the houses on the lane are midnight-hushed—
all but mine, with its boisterous exuberance
and late-ringing chords, its minor key.

Daughter

You like to tell the story of your childhood—
how I would close the door each afternoon
and light the white candle, trying to believe

the candle's tiny flame was the only real thing
in this fleeting universe of illusions and dreams.
Remember how at midnight I'd stand out back

in the dew under the moon and sing very softly
a song about home and how home doesn't exist?
It must have been hard for you, watching me

at my black typewriter, striking the keys as if I were
trying to extinguish a fire or maybe something
worse that was burning inside me, if *burning's*

the word, all ashes and waste. It's true: I was never
satisfied, many balled-up sheets of paper piled high
around my desk like snow that would have buried me

in great white drifts of time and meaninglessness
had you not been there to gather the sad drafts
and throw them by the armful in the fireplace.

Patience

I beguiled my wife and daughter to join me
for a picnic on a blanket by the pretty river.
I was seeking a nineteenth-century feeling
and let all desire drift on the river's soft silk

while my wife spoke in low whispers like a sibyl
and our daughter dreamed beneath the trees.
To answer the enigma and mystery of life,
I thought of opening my yellow sketchbook

and drawing the willows over the banks
and my daughter's hands folded in prayer,
but no charcoal sketch can solve this riddle.
One cannot even ask such questions aloud,

for the most judicious words only break the spell.
Instead, it must be enough—my wife's green eyes,
our daughter drowsing on our checked blanket,
the river's veiled and quiet song.

Painting at Night

On a clear night I go outside
to paint the stars, blue Rigel
and yellow-red Arcturus,
erecting my easel and canvas
in the dark, navy and cobalt
deepening like the sky until
I can't see the brushstrokes.
Then I paint the shiny specks
twinkling above, white dots
I can hardly see in the dark
unless I make big circles.
Then I've painted the moon
in the center of the canvas,
a moon reflecting the light
I never believe existed
before I became a painter—
the light shining from my face.

Youth

Now that I have grown old,
I have the gift of becoming
invisible. Or maybe it's that
I know how to be a stone.
Either way, some days I stand
perfectly still with my eyes closed
in the foyer of Arts & Letters Hall
right when all the classes let out
and all the young students waterfall
down the broad staircase and
spill forth from the elevators
and swim the hallway's currents,
all of them hurrying for the door
that will release them back out
into the world, even though
I stand in their way, an obstacle,
perfectly still, invisible, unseen,
like a big rock in the middle of
a roaring river, the tumbling water
rushing by me without a thought.

The Photographer

My father was a good photographer—
I still have his Leica and his Kodak
and old tins filled with black and whites
of Egypt, the Philippines, Burma,
pictures of the pyramids and camels
and the straw huts he lived in
when he was in the Pacific,
the automobiles of his youth,
my mother on horseback in Carolina,
and the occasional self-portrait
in which he appears in uniform
by a fighter plane called *The Valiant*.
His photograph of the Taj Mahal,
which he took during World War II,
feels like an unblemished miracle to me,
more mystical than the palace itself.
And this one of winter trees in snow—
austere in its black-and-white beauty—
he must have taken as a young man
somewhere in America, I think,
with a camera that is now lost to time.
Looking through my father's photographs—
the places often unknown and I
unable to ask, now that he's gone—
I become keenly aware of life's mystery.

The Study

Summer nights when I can't sleep,
I go downstairs to sit by the open window in the study.

I turn on the lamp, take a book from the shelf,
sit in my comfy chair, and soon find myself

listening to the crickets singing outside,
that choir in the grass,

the humming that enchants and delights.
Nothing competes with a chorus of katydids—

open books can only rest quiet in my lap,
as if they too

enjoyed the entrancing sound of peace.
To better hear, I turn out my lamp

and sit for a long while by the window in the dark—
books closed, eyes closed, all of us listening.

fin

About the Author

Richard Jones is the author of several books of poetry, including *Country of Air*, *The Blessing*, *Apropos of Nothing*, *Stranger on Earth*, and *Avalon*. He is also the award-winning editor of *Poetry East* and over the last four decades has curated its many anthologies, including *The Last Believer in Words*, *Bliss*, *Origins*, *Wider than the Sky*, and *London*.